ISSN 2572-6706 (print)
ISSN 2572-6714 (online)

IABS Journal

Independent Association of Business Scholars

Edition 2 Volume 1

July 2017

Editor in Chief	*Dr. J. Robert Heinzman*
Editor	*Dr. Brian A. Iannucci*
Website	www.iabs-publishing.com

EDITORS NOTE

In this volume of IABS, we have gathered articles discussing morality and intent, new ideas about career services focus for college graduates, and Global Leadership.

Dr. Heinzman provides views of perception based on ethical and moral focus. An individual may or may not be driven by altruistic purposes. In his piece on Candlelight Philosophy, he explores intent. The intent for a positive purpose may meet personal morals but may not be perceived by the receiver as moral.

Dr. Iannucci provides a timely discussion on career services and the challenges facing them in today's environment. Individuals who have left the work force and are returning have little assistance in finding jobs. These individuals look to education to prepare them for today's work force only to be let down by the poor career services provided by colleges traditional career services. In this piece, Dr. Iannucci provides a fresh idea on how to address society's needs today.

Dr. Perez provides an overview of leadership practices needed in a global organization. Within this article, we find several characteristics and practices for leading teams and creating an appreciative work environment.

Certainly, a diverse wealth of material which I believe has great value for any who read this material with a thoughtful purpose.

May ignorance be left behind and rhetoric melt away.

Dr. J. Robert Heinzman

Candlelight Philosophy

Joseph Robert Heinzman D. M.

jrheinzman@yahoo.com

Abstract

The ideals of ethics and morality depend on intent. We have choices which are driven by our beliefs and morals, we may either do good or evil. Is society driven by Nietzsche's idea of levels of bad or more idealistic and moral. What is morality, is it as Kant theorized, moral is carrying out the intention of what the individual states. Bakhtin theorized that ethics and norms are based on an interplay of known and anticipated actions. Business organizations must be cognizant of direction and perception of the public to their actions. Corporate Social Responsibility is not just a statement it is the reality of the organization's values and norms.

Keywords: Values, Perception, Kant, Ethics, Morals, Transparency

Does a candle burn brightest when lit or does it have moments where the light comes and goes? I am sitting here watching the flicker of the candle and realize at the beginning the light was great but as it burns on the intensity does not change. There are moments where it sputters, the light seems to dim and then it burns brighter as if alive and breathing. These moments bring about some lucidity of thought which causes me to ponder my existence and purpose in actions and deeds.

Am I at the end the beginning or in between, but where on the candle am I, might be a better question toward who I am and my purpose? Am I at a point of brightness or am I to the point of dimming or sputtering trying to decide a new path, a different opportunity, or just continue the way I am now? I can't be the only one who contemplates existence at a level so inconceivably insignificant that the effort seems to be painful. Nietzsche posited that there is no evil, only levels of bad. Morality is a moment of decision, based on values we have learned, or experienced, which fits our cultural norms. Is a man evil because he kicks a dog? Some would say yes, while others will ask why he kicked the dog.

I sit here at a crossroads of values and norms and ask myself what brings me to this point, why should I care about my neighbor if my neighbor does not care about me. Why should you care about why I kicked the dog, or why I decided I no longer wanted a tree, a bush, or flower in my yard? Who are you to interfere in my existence if my existence didn't matter a moment ago, did that tree hold a meaning for you, and if it did, why didn't you help keep it from the fate which caused its removal?

I'm not going to tell you the tree deserved to die, to make me seem correct, I'm not going to say anything, other than it needed to go. Our actions and inactions seem to have import when someone takes notice and interferes with our direction. Is interplay what reality is, are norms the clash of values continuously interfering with each other until one wins over? Bakhtin (1993) might call this the interplay between dominant and societal ethics. The interplay of traditional interactions and influence based on a societal norm creating a base of values.

When I think about the morals behind win-win and win-lose scenarios, think when is the last time you lost a fight with yourself? The only time we lose is when the decision has a painful outcome. Pain comes in many forms, monetary, psychological, spiritual, and actual physical pain. Society has driven a wedge so deeply entrenched in its own cultural bias no one knows who is the moral man. Dialogism (Bakhtin, 1993) theorizes that language and certain works of literature exist in a dynamic state. How we address a conversation or an event is based on events which have occurred and in anticipation of how others will respond.

Another small item to realize is the use of gender form in my writing, I defer to the traditional form where the term "man" stands for human be it women or man, black, white, yellow, pink, Christian, Muslim, Buddhist, or anywhere in between. I am not here to pass judgment or to claim a problem exist past the reality of social consequences of others enacting their will upon others. Ethically, actions should be in line with a stated policy. An organization who claims to focus on the public good, but acts in opposition through separate policies may be considered immoral. Kantian logic would identify actions opposite to stated policy as parasitic (Sullivan, 1989).

Why am I writing any of this at all? Today I sit here like the candle partially burnt out, not as bright, dimming and wondering if I will have another spark which will spur me forth into consequence again. I am not sure if life is a moment or a series of moments when we have the opportunity to burn bright and make a difference. In my action will I interfere or will I make things better? Better for whom, others or myself. Is it that underpinning response to feeling worth that drives us to get involved? Is involvement a need to connect to others or show worth beyond ourselves? Maybe the action is to prove our value is more than someone else, that could be where the level of bad really begins to show that morality is only our own perception based on our own self-absorbed reality.

My purpose, so I thought, was to be a part of society in a manner to create a kinder gentler world. In the process of travels, I have found people are people and we all want the same thing, to live and enjoy the existence we believe in. Being transparent is about being true, building trust and setting a clear moral example.

Maybe that is where we should begin, how did you come to this moment and why? When presented with choices what moments defined your true self? When looking for what an individual moves toward, stress is a great indicator. When presented with a challenge, that is beyond our immediate knowledge of possible outcomes, we have to make choices of actionable responses. What is your directional compass telling you, are you looking for win-win, win-lose, lose-lose, or is it just not worth the time?

Why did you kick the dog? Why did you drink the last glass of milk? Why am I still reading this and why should I care? Simple questions, complex answers, unless maybe we can overcome our own self-absorbed notions of cultural values and inclination to force our will on others. Life is a series of questions at those moments of decision, we can reignite the candle of life and keep it from sputtering into obscurity. I'm tired and the reason I am sitting here writing is still not clear, so I will share my moment and hope it allows some peace for now.

Today my son had an incident where he crashed his car and totaled it. I do not share this for pity or remorse, he is unharmed although without a car now. The point is he was working hard to earn money and continue his journey forward. My first reaction was not the altruistic man I would like to be, although I did attempt to come to the rescue and assist him. Isn't that what a father should do? My wife helped me to keep my sanity. Isn't that what spouses are for? The end result I helped him by being there, providing a means to tow the car, and ensuring he is now home safe. The end result, he is without a car but he is safe. Let me share the interesting part of what has kept me up tonight.

The accident and loss of my sons means to freedom and earning a living. When my wife and I arrived at the scene of the accident, in front of a car dealer, he is inside the establishment waiting. The dealership has made an offer to tow his car for free. At first thought you are thinking what a morally correct thing to do, but not so fast. The point of discussion that has occurred with my son is that they would be willing to tow it if he was interested in buying a used car.

Ethically it is a noble gesture to tow the car for free, but only if the cost can be absorbed through the sale of a vehicle. From a deontological viewpoint the right thing for the dealership is to help but at the same time, they have an obligation to sell cars. The auto dealer is not in the business of charity. From an ethical standpoint based in Kantian deontology, the right or wrong of the consequence which would be my son having a car loan is not bad, although it does not achieve a vehicle without a car payment, the original state before the accident.

The next offer from the Auto Dealer Manager was if my son was interested in a job, they could sell him a car and he would have a new job. The Kantian logic here would indicate a level of moral duty in the combination of acts in trying to provide my son a method to have a vehicle and income. The point here being they need people to work, he needs a job, and with income maybe we can buy a car.

Conclusion

Again back to levels of bad based on our perception of values and ethical conclusions. Organizations must be aware of how their statements and actions drive perception. Business morality can drive away customers if the value of the business is not perceived as ethical. Back to the beginning where I wondered why we interfere with one another, maybe it is compassion, connection, self-sense of worth, or a combination of moments where the candle burns bright then sputters and brightens again. Each of us must keep in mind our actions upon others and the result upon the organization. As leaders, we must be the ethical role model, transparent is not just a word. The historical actions and the anticipation of coming events may cause a negative outcome if a leader, and the organization, is not transparent. Without transparency trust, morality, and ethics may fail.

References

Bakhtin, M. (1993). *Toward a Philosophy of the Act*. University of Texas Press, Austin.

Sullivan, R.J. (1989). *Immanuel Kant's Moral Theory*. Cambridge University Press, Cambridge.

Creating a Sustainable Nationwide Career Services Model: Meeting Students' Needs in a Changing Employment Environment

Brian A. Iannucci, Ph.D., MBA

Abstract

In examining the current best practices in higher education regarding career services and placement post-graduation this article endeavors to clearly define the problem facing higher education in this aspect as well as proposes some solutions that could be implemented in order to better serve the needs to students, graduates, and alumni regarding job placement and gainful employment after graduation and beyond as they continue through their career. The author presents this as a beginning point to the discussion in the hopes that this article might be a catalyst for future change and improvement to this aspect of the higher education model currently in place in the United States.

Keywords: Career Services, Higher Education, Traditional Ed.

One fact, above all others, is a unifying quality that students who are enrolling in higher education share (Watts, 2006). That fact is simply that they seek to improve their prospects for career and professional success. Very few students enroll in an education without some aspiration of career growth. Given this fact it is important to keep in mind the needs of students both during and after graduation.

In recent years there has been an emphasis on preparing students and providing education that meets the needs of the profession in which they aspire to engage. This, rightly so, has been a lofty goal and to this end, many universities have made a marked improvement. Through partnerships with industry professionals, benchmarking skills, and advisory boards, education has been modified and enhanced to more properly prepare graduates for the rigors they will encounter in their field.

However, the needs of students after graduation are woefully underserved. This is a fact that has not been lost on the higher education industry for years and was even noted in the literature nearly forty years ago (Reardon, Zunker, and Dyal, 1979). Linking qualified graduates with professional opportunities and careers within their chosen fields has been a challenge. Additionally, there are demographic and geographic issues at play with the changing face of the student body at many universities. Students and graduates are coming from a broader cross section of the population. In years past the vast majority of students and graduates were beginning their careers in their early to mid-twenties. Now we are seeing the mean age of graduates increasing and a number of students choosing to go back to school for a myriad of reasons. These reasons most often are to gain skills that will allow them to reenter and compete in the workforce. These non-traditional students include former stay-at-home parents seeking to reenter the workforce after their children have reached adulthood, individuals who are in careers that have been downsized or replaced with technology, or simply those who seek to change careers. To be certain, the days when one was employed by the same company for thirty plus years are gone. Career change is a fact of life and education has been tasked with keeping up with this societal change. There is a definite need for an enhanced approach to career services within higher education in order to meet their needs. In order to more successfully link graduates to their chosen careers, it will be necessary to revisit our current approach.

Within this short discussion, the needs of graduates will be defined as well as solutions proposed to address these needs. Further, given the recent emphasis placed on job placement within the education industry, it is important to note that it will be important to continue this discussion as new opportunities present themselves. In short, this is only the beginning of our conversation.

Defining the Problem

Currently, the education industry is focused on their present role of preparing students for their various fields. This preparation includes defining curriculum objectives, preparing learning resources, developing assessments, and benchmarking all aspects of this process to other universities as well as the industries to which the field feeds. This is an important undertaking and, as noted previously, great strides have been made to increase alignment and success. The role of traditional education has also been supplemented by other models of education that include universities and colleges with a national scope, competency-based models, online curriculums, and other innovations. All of these have added to the tapestry of higher education and their impact has provided a market influence that has spurred growth, access, and innovation. Ultimately these have helped to expand high-quality educational options for perspective students that allow them to tailor their educational careers in order to better meet their needs. Traditional higher education has made attempts to provide career connection for the student but regularly falls short. This has left many graduates largely on their own when seeking employment opportunities within their field. Students have been provided little or no support from career services departments. This has been due to a myriad of issues; not the least of which is the lack of funding for such departments at traditional institutions.

In the end, students are tasked with finding their own career opportunities without the assistance of their affiliated institutions. The impact has been that many students are not prepared to seek out and obtain the very careers they have been trained to undertake. This has been a source of frustration within higher education. Recently, many states, such as Florida, have been awarding funding for institutions that demonstrate a higher than average placement of students in their fields and gainful employment laws have had the effect of placing an emphasis on placement. This emphasis has led to a furtherance of this discussion and has deemed this article apropos and germane to the current educational climate.

Nationally accredited schools, largely driven by the proprietary, for-profit sector of higher education, have also provided an emphasis on career education specifically with modular and certificate programs. This has helped to supplement fields such as medical assisting, pharmacy technician, and various trades. While the obvious problems in the for-profit model are evident these schools have had an increased focus on job placement when compared to their regionally accredited competitors. This emphasis stems largely from the accreditation bodies' focus on placement as a measure for accreditation and re-accreditation.

For this reason, these institutions have expended budget resources to develop local relationships in order to place students in their chosen fields. It is from this model that higher education, in general, can learn. Further, this model can be used as a stepping off point for other educational institutions.

In addition to the contrast between regionally and nationally accredited institutions, it is important to note the increase in online education options that have confounded the problem of career services as their student base is broadly spread out throughout the nation and beyond. This creates a difficult conundrum for such institutions as it exponentially increases the geographic area that the institution must cover when seeking career opportunities for graduates. Given the increase in such institutions, as well as the mobility of students from a variety of universities seeking employment beyond the geographic footprint of current institutions, the remainder of this discussion will focus on ideas for creating a sustainable and effective model for a national career services effort.

It is important to note that any solution which will effectively address this problem must include the following:

1. A strategic nationwide approach to targeting career services that will allow students in all fifty states, and beyond, an opportunity to receive assistance with placement services post-graduation.

2. The establishment of targeted, regional and state-based partnerships between companies and the educational institution such that students can be trained to meet the needs of both the industry as well as the particular companies.

3. The establishment of regional and state-based career service departments that are tasked with cultivating relationships with both graduates as well as companies within their geographic scope.

4. Value-added services such as resume assistance, soft skills education, interviewing skills, post-graduate support, and career fairs that entice students and graduates to engage in the system.

5. The establishment of a value proposition for companies in order to gain their participation. This includes providing educational opportunities within the organization, providing qualified and screened applicants for positions, and strategic partnerships regarding future needs in regards to skills and staffing.

6. Research has shown that technology has been shown to be a great benefit for students, recent graduates, and alumni as it pertains to career services (Venable, 2010). Therefore, a push should be made to provide asynchronous and synchronous technological resources to meet this need and further entice use and engagement on behalf of students, recent graduates, and alumni.

Creating a Solution

The current model of cursory career services must be augmented. Currently, many institutions have focused on basic skills and services such as resume writing and have left it up to the individual student to seek employment opportunities that meet their specific needs. This has led to students seeking opportunities using job boards, websites, and personal networking to the extent they are able. Overall the frustration in finding gainful employment after graduation has led many students to be frustrated and even to elect to enroll in further education thus prolonging and putting off the need to find employment. This has led to an even more highly educated workforce that is seeking positions. While the short-term gain of enrollment is enticing for many institutions the inevitability of having graduates who are ill-equipped to find gainful employment, many of whom face mounting pressure to repay student loans, is a frightening thought.

Instead of the current model, there is an opportunity for increased success with the proper organization and focus. It is proposed that institutions establish regional and state-based career service director positions and departments that will work along side of alumni efforts. The focus of each directorship/department should be to build a team of human resource and sales professionals responsible for the following:

1. Developing relationships with graduates and alumni within their geographic scope in order to support efforts in preparing for and finding gainful employment. These efforts should include regular, localized alumni events where the value-added would be to provide further education in job sourcing, interviewing, soft skills, and resume development. This will lead to the creation of a database of qualified alumni for a myriad of positions. It is important to note that this goal can be aligned with current alumni effort and a synergy within the institution may be found. This internal partnership may benefit this effort and should be explored.

In addition, technological resources should be implemented in order to provide career services benefits to students, graduates, and alumni in order to better meet the needs of this population. Further, these resources will help to bridge the gap with students who are not close to their "brick and mortar" campus.

2. Developing relationships with large companies who are currently or will be at some point in the future hiring within the geographic region and actively partnering with human resource departments to place students within these organizations. Further, these partnerships will serve a dual purpose of increasing awareness of the institution. This partnership may also allow for further opportunity to expand educational offerings and collaborations between the institution and the partner organization that is exclusive to the partner organization; possibly at a discount and/or on-site. This would create a win/win situation as the partnership would benefit the institution in the way of placement, recognition, and increased enrollment. Further, this partnership would benefit the partner company by providing qualified and trained applicants, educational opportunities, and the opportunity to have major input in the creation of curriculum to better prepare students for their organization. Research has shown that universities are still viewed as a major source for hiring individuals for professional and managerial positions (Ng & Burke, 2006).

3. Establish partnerships with local hospitals, school districts, and other programmatically specific organizations such as SHRM, CPA, and other professional associations, as well as various

business groups such as the Better Business Bureau and Chambers of Commerce. These relationships will provide many of the same benefits as those seen in the previous objective and further expand the scope of the institution's efforts.

4. Develop scholarship opportunities geared toward assisting students in the designated geographic areas to develop skills that match employment needs regionally. These efforts could include fields such as nursing, education, specific business needs such as logistics, as well as many others that could be defined as a regional knowledge of the employment landscape is strategically evaluated.

5. Partnering with feeder institutions such as community colleges in order to provide further educational opportunities for students.

Overall, these efforts would provide the broad-based approach necessary to meet the needs of graduates and alumni. By coordinating with the various stakeholders that are impacted after students' graduation and providing an intentional connection between them, such partnerships will benefit all involved. These efforts will allow for increased success for students as they will enhance employment prospects as well as the recognition of their alma mater. From an institutional perspective, the benefits include enhanced recognition, increased enrollment, established trust, and industry support. For the various companies and external stakeholders, the benefits include a trained workforce that meets their needs going forward, a voice in the development of new curriculum and programs, and the opportunity to further job training at an institution with whom they have an established relationship.

In short, this proposal is a WIN-WIN!

Conclusion

The current conditions within higher education point to the fact that the current system of connecting graduates to employment is flawed and even broken. There is a need for a more deliberate and well thought out system of career services at an institutional level. The establishment of such a systematic approach to finding a solution as prescribed previously would yield benefits for many stakeholders and will ultimately create a more effective transition from student to graduate to gainful employment.

To be certain, the goals set forth previously are lofty. In order to address them, a tactical approach will be necessary. This sort of approach will incur cost and will necessarily mean a paradigm shift within every institution. However, it cannot be forgotten that this approach does have several benefits to the institution as well as the various stakeholders.

It has now become the burden of each of us to continue this conversation. Our task is not to simply remain satisfied with the status quo. Rather, it is to build a better system that can benefit all involved.

Finally, it is now our turn to make a lasting impact on higher education by seeing that those who have had the benefit of its lessons go on to employ those lessons for the benefit of themselves and society. For, at its core, isn't that the true goal of higher education?

References

Ng, E. S., & Burke, R. J. (2006). The next generation at work–business students' views, values and job search strategy: Implications for universities and employers. *Education+ Training*, *48*(7), 478-492.

Reardon, R., Zunker, V., & Dyal, M. A. (1979). The status of career planning programs and career centers in colleges and universities. *The Career Development Quarterly*, *28*(2), 154-159.

Venable, M. A. (2010). Using technology to deliver career development services: Supporting today's students in higher education. *The career development quarterly*, *59*(1), 87-96.

Watts, A. G. (2006). Career development learning and employability.

21st-Century Global Leadership and Beyond

By

Jose Perez
jperez@coloradotech.edu

Colorado Technical University
4435 N. Chestnut Street
Colorado Springs, CO 80907

Abstract

The business world is expanding. Much of this growth is being driven by globalization and advances in technology. The characteristics and practices which helped organizational leaders to succeed just a few decades ago have changed. The purpose of this paper was to examine the characteristics and practices essential for leading global organizations today and well into the future. This paper also addresses several characteristics and practices essential for leading global teams, managing conflict, and diversity. A discussion of how these characteristics and practices help organizations to maintain a competitive edge was also provided. However, a review of the literature uncovered a gap in future research to be focused on how to evaluate and develop a global mindset at the organizational level.

Key words: *Transcultural Leadership, Cross-Cultural Leadership, Multiculturalism, Global Leadership*

The global business market is growing. Globalization and the leveraging of technology is driving much of this growth. With this growth, comes the opportunity to expand operations internationally. For those organizations that decide to jump into the global business landscape, there will be new markets to discover. There will also be challenges associated with entering those markets. However, the type of leadership approaches which were responsible for achieving success domestically may not apply in a global context. This is because the global environment is complicated. Leading globally requires leaders to possess certain characteristics essential for leading today's global organizations. Today's and tomorrow's leaders will also need to be able to apply leadership in a manner that takes into consideration the multicultural compositions of their organizations. The ability to lead diverse teams and manage conflict will also be essential for organizational success. This will demand leaders who are skillful at leading complex global systems and organizations. These leaders will also need to have the attributes necessary for distinguishing them as global leaders.

Problem Statement

Globalization has created many challenges for 21st-century global leaders. For example, differences between cultures, political ideologies, and even religion demand that today's global leaders be sensitive and familiar with the world around them. Lack of sensitivity to such factors can be catastrophic to the bottom line for global organizations. As a result, leading a global organization requires special knowledge and skills. This paper will examine the characteristics and practices essential for leading global organizations today and well into the future. This paper will also address those characteristics and practices essential for leading global teams, managing conflict, and diversity, which helps them maintain their competitive edge.

Literature Review

As globalization continues to increase, it is creating opportunities for many businesses to expand their operations internationally. The leaders who will lead these organizations will need to have the characteristics and practices essential for leading global organizations today and well into the future. According to Mendenhall (2013), there are three key sets of global leadership skills which are distinctive for leading an international organization. The first is the wisdom and expertise to lead their organizations. The second is the ability to manage people and form meaningful relationships. The third is the capability to manage self. Forsyth (2015) postulates that 21st-century global leaders will need to demonstrate several characteristics if they are to succeed today and in the future. For example, cultural intelligence, being a lifelong learner, strategic thinking, and strong communications skills are just a few of the characterizes needed for being a successful global leader, according to Forsyth.

Furthermore, Caldwell (2015) identified five universally accepted characteristics of leadership which was found among organizations that excelled in their industries. The five characteristics identified were (a) constant organizational development, (b) results driven, (c) a quality leadership team, (d) a diverse workforce, and (e) a future-oriented mindset about organizational goals. According to Caldwell, these five factors have a direct influence on how well a leader will be able to lead a global organization.

Looking towards the future, Povah (2012) distinguished five basic characteristics of leadership which will be needed by future leaders. First, leaders will need to have the intellectual capacity to lead. Second, they will need to have high levels of emotional intelligence. Third, tomorrow's leaders will need to have strong moral values. Also, leaders will need to have the drive and resilience to reach their goals. Finally, they must be willing to learn from their experiences. However, Povah adds that all these are mute if the leader does not fit into the organization's culture. These basic characteristics must be aligned with the organization's mission, values, and vision of its future if the leader is ever expected to succeed, according to Povah.

Research conducted by Cseh, Davis, and Khilji (2013) identified that a leader's intellectual, psychological, and social abilities were critical components for developing a global mindset. According to Cseh, Davis, and Khilji, these three important components can be integrated to help leaders develop a global mindset. Therefore, it can be argued that with the right training and support, leaders of international organizations can develop a global mindset and become good global leaders (Minner, 2015).

For any organization to succeed it requires teamwork. This facet of leadership is even more critical in a global organization because of the number of people it takes to work together to achieve a common goal. These common goals cannot be achieved without teamwork on a global scale. This requires good leadership. There are characteristics and practices leaders need to effectively lead global teams. According to Mendenhall (2013), there are several common characteristics that are shared by effective global teams. One characteristic of effective global teams is clearly defined tasks and goals. Here each team member understands his or her role and holds themselves accountable for achieving those goals. Another characteristic of global teams is that they are diverse with the right combination of skills needed to complete their tasks. Mendenhall further adds that effective global teams respect and trust each other as well as their cultural differences. Matthews and McLees (2015) argue that leaders who create a team culture of trust and mutual respect helps increase teamwork and leads to improved organizational performance.

Dumitrescu, Lie, and Dobrescu (2014) also identified several characteristics and practices of successful global teams. Since most global teams are culturally diverse, global leaders must respect this multicultural diversity. Global leaders should also be able to speak and understand a foreign language in addition to their domestic language. Global leaders must also recognize that each team member has a different learning style and each impacts team performance. Dumitrescu, Lie, and Dobrescu further add that leaders who lead global teams must also be empathetic towards their team members. Therefore, these leadership characteristics and practices have a role in creating effective global teams.

Essentials for Global Conflict Management

The fact that global organizations are highly diverse, it is inevitable that conflicts will occur. It is not a matter of if it will occur, but when it will happen. When they do occur, leaders must be ready to resolve them quickly to minimize the disruption they create to maintain organizational performance. Therefore, global leaders must understand the characteristics and practices essential for successfully managing organizational conflict. Thomas and Kilmann (Prause & Mujtaba, 2015) described five conflict management practices leaders use to handle conflict in diverse organizations, which can also be applied to global organizations. The first approach is referred to as competing because the leader uses his or her formal authority to force the desired outcome. The second approach uses accommodating conflict management in which there is one clear winner at the expense of the other person. The third conflict management approach is called avoiding because the leader ignores the conflict situation in hopes that it will go away. The fourth conflict management approach is a collaboration where the leader creates a win-win situation which satisfies both parties. This is the preferred method for resolving a conflict. The last approach is compromising where the leader attempts to resolve the conflict in a manner that is partially satisfactory to both individuals. According to Thomas and Kilmann, this last approach is often a temporary solution.

Organizational leaders are tasked with creating a harmonious workplace, which leads to improved performance. However, conflicts do occur. When they do occur, leadership styles can influence conflict management outcomes. Research studies have shown that there is a relationship between leadership styles and conflict management practices. For example, Saeed, Almas, Anis-ul-Haq, and Niazi (2014) studied 150 mid-level managers and found that their leadership styles were a factor in how they managed conflict. Their study showed that transformational leadership was effective for most conflict management situations because transformational leaders were likely to be more open minded and use obligating styles of conflict management. Conversely, transactional leadership was associated with the compromising conflict management approach, while laissez-fair leadership was associated with the avoiding conflict management approach. The implication for global leaders is that if they are to effectively manage conflict, they must understand that their leadership styles influence their conflict management choices.

Essentials for Global Diversity

The workplace of the 21st-century is changing. There is a demographic shift occurring. There are now multiple generations working together in the workplace. Woman employees comprise a larger share of the workforce than they did several decades ago. Globalization is also introducing new cultures into the workplace. For organizations to succeed in this environment they will need leaders who have the ability to lead a diverse workplace. Leaders will need to create an environment where employees feel valued and can contribute to the success of the organization (Derven, 2014). In fact, leaders will need to learn to manage diversity and the many cultural differences that exist in the workplace (Sharma, 2016). Sharma (2016) further adds that diversity management will require leaders to encourage diversity and develop a culture of inclusiveness so the organization can achieve maximum performance. Also, according to Smith (2015), leaders who can manage diversity are equipped with the tools necessary for minimizing or eliminating potential conflicts within the organization.

There are essential practices leaders can implement to successfully manage organizational diversity. For example, Verma (2015) identified five essential strategic practices leaders could apply for managing diversity.

First, senior leadership must support a culture of diversity. Unless senior leadership embraces the value of diversity, any diversity management effort will fail. Second, there must be human resource plans in place for creating policies and practices that support diversity such as recruitment and retention efforts. Third, to help employees better understand diversity and its value, there must be training in place to educate employees about the importance and value diversity adds to the organizations. The organization must also periodically conduct organizational assessments to uncover any potential bias to any group within the organization. There must also be effective communication systems in place so information regarding promoting diversity can be disseminated. Finally, there must be consistent monitoring and accountability of diversity efforts to ensure its success. Collectively, these practices help create an environment which will allow leaders to manage organizational diversity more effectively.

Putting it Together to Maintain a Competitive Edge

A review of the literature showed that the characteristics and practices previously discussed were necessary for leading global organizations. Likewise, these characteristics and practices also assist global organizations in maintaining their competitive edge. For example, wisdom and expertise allow global leaders to develop strategies and visions necessary for sustaining the organization in the long-term. Managing people and building relationships produce loyalty and enable leaders to effectively collaborate with numerous stakeholders in their efforts to accomplish the organization's strategic objectives (Mendenhall, 2013). When leaders are reflective, they are more purposeful about how their behavior affects organizational outcomes.

Leaders who adopt the attitude of continuously developing and improving the organization build a culture that is willing to accept change. This provides a competitive edge because it allows for more flexibility in an already turbulent environment. Also, by embracing diversity, leaders create an environment that permits organizational members to respect each other's differences. This is essential for building a bridge of understanding across multiple cultures (Caldwell, 2015). Furthermore, being open to diversity and its role in a global organization, facilitates team building practices and minimizes the conflicts which ultimately arise due to group differences. Also, being aware of the different conflict management practices described by Prause and Mujtaba (2015) helps maintain a competitive advantage by helping to avoid any unnecessary disruptions which may prevent the organization from achieving its objectives.

While all these characteristics and practices help maintain a competitive edge, they must be accomplished by leaders who have or can develop a global mindset. Doing so allows global leaders to sustain their competitive edge in the 21st-century and beyond. According to Cseh, Davis, and Khilji (2013), a global mindset is a holistic approach to leading globally. This creates a competitive edge because leaders can combine these characteristics and practices and apply them both domestically and globally to accomplish the organization's goals. Therefore, when organization leaders put all these facets together, they can maintain a competitive edge.

Summary

The business world is expanding. Much of this growth is being driven by globalization and advances in technology. The characteristics and practices which helped organizational leaders to succeed just a few decades ago have changed. The new leadership paradigm now requires leaders to have a global mindset. This will require special leadership abilities related to our global environment to succeed in the 21st-century and beyond. This paper examined the characteristics and practices essential for leading global organizations today and well into the future. This paper also addressed several characteristics and practices essential for leading global teams, managing conflict, and diversity. A discussion of how these characteristics and practices assist organizations to maintain a competitive edge was also provided.

Recommendations and Conclusion

To prepare leaders to lead in the 21st-century and beyond will require careful thought and planning. The world has become smaller and global markets more competitive as developing countries enter the international business arena. This has resulted in a more integrated and complex global system. To navigate this terrain, leaders will need to develop a global mindset. They will also need to have the right characteristics and apply leadership practices that take into consideration the diversity inherent in their organizations along with the complexities found in the business world. Therefore, to facilitate the development of global leaders, it is recommended that organizations better prepare their leaders to become global leaders. This can be accomplished by providing evidenced-based leadership training. Training and development in improving cultural intelligence is also essential. This training can be formal as well as informal. Individuals who have been identified as potential global leaders can also be given expatriate leadership assignments to provide them with the necessary experience for developing a global mindset. This will also help increase their cultural intelligence. Human resource management departments will also need to play a more strategic role in the leadership development process. For example, they can develop policies that support diversity and inclusiveness. Hiring and retention policies that support the importance of diversity management are examples. Finally, senior leadership must lead by example. They must create a culture which is empathetic and fosters a global mindset.

In conclusion, a review of the literature showed that there are several characteristics and practices essential for leading global organizations today and into the future. Wisdom, the ability to build meaningful relationships, and strategic thinking were a few characteristics and practices needed to succeed as a global leader. Leading teams, the ability to manage diversity, and manage conflict were also found to be necessary for leading in the 21st-century and beyond. Leaders who exhibited these qualities also help their organizations maintain a competitive edge. Finally, by developing and training their future leaders, organizations can create a pipeline of ready and capable leaders to help sustain themselves well into the future. However, a review of the literature uncovered a gap in future research to be focused on how to evaluate and develop a global mindset at the organizational level.

References

Caldwell, J. (2015). Leading globally, thinking interculturally: Developing global characteristics. *The Journal of Business Diversity, 15*(1), 55-59.

Cseh, M., Davis, E. B., & Khilji, S. E. (2013). Developing a global mindset: Learning of global leaders. *European Journal of Training and Development, 37*(5), 489-499.

Derven, M. (2014). Diversity and inclusion by design: Best practices from six global companies. *Industrial and Commercial Training, 46*(2), 84-91.

Dumitrescu, C. I., Lie, I. R., & Dobrescu, R. M. (2014). Leading Multicultural Teams. *FAIMA Business & Management Journal, 2*(4), 43-54. Retrieved from

Forsyth, B. (2015). Characteristics and practices essential to leading global organizations in the 21st century. *Journal of Management Policy and Practice, 16*(1), 108-117.

Matthews, R., & McLees, J. (2015). Building effective projects teams and teamwork. *Journal of Information Technology and Economic Development, 6*(2), 20-30.

Mendenhall, M. E. (2013). *Global leadership: Research, practice, and development* [Vitalsource] (2nd ed.).

Minner, W. (2015). Leading global organizations. *Journal of Management Policy and Practice, 16*(2), 122-126.

Povah, L. (2012). Assessing leaders for the future. *Industrial and Commercial Training, 44*(5), 250-258.

Prause, D., & Mujtaba, B. G. (2015). Conflict management practices for diverse workplaces. *Journal of Business Studies Quarterly, 6*(3), 13-22.

Saeed, T., Almas, S., Anis-ul-Haq, M., & Niazi, G. (2014). Leadership styles: Relationship with conflict management styles. *International Journal of Conflict Management, 25*(3), 214-225.

Sharma, U. (2016). Managing diversity and cultural differences at the workplace. *IPE Journal of Management, 6*(2), 63-79. Retrieved from

Smith, D. L. (2015). Benchmarking global leadership. *Journal of Leadership, Accountability and Ethics, 12*(3), 113-118.

Verma, A. (2015). Valuing diversity: Strategies and implications for organizational success. *Prestige International Journal of Management and Research, 7/8*(2), 31-38.

Author Information / Submission Guidelines

Authors are invited to submit theoretical and empirical papers in all categories of business such as e-business, general management, international business, strategy, marketing, supply chain management, organization studies, entrepreneurship, enterprise, innovation and human resource management. This list is not meant to be exhaustive, but rather an indication of the areas of concern of the journal.

We welcome paper submissions on the basis that the material has not been published elsewhere. We also aim to develop a journal that will appeal to both business and management practitioners. On that basis, papers that include practical applications to any business and management field are welcomed.

We endeavor to provide rapid and informative feedback to authors. Our objective is to obtain peer reviews from referees within 10 weeks of the initial paper submission. We are looking forward to receiving quality submissions for our forthcoming volumes.

Please go to: *https://www.iabs-publishing.com/contact* for submission, subscribe, and for information on submission guidelines.